SpongeBob SquarePants™

ANOTHER DAY, ANOTHER SAND DOLLAR

Contributing Editor - Kimberlee Smith & Dave Schreiber
Graphic Design and Lettering - Tomás Montalvo-Lagos & Monalisa J. de Asis
Cover Layout - Raymond Makowski
Graphic Artist - Jennifer Nunn-Iwai

Editor - Jod Kaftan
Digital Imaging Manager - Chris Buford
Pre-Press Manager - Antonio DePietro
Production Manager - Jennifer Miller
Art Director - Matt Alford
Managing Editor - Jill Freshney
Editorial Director - Jeremy Ross
VP of Production - Ron Klamert
President & C.O.O. - John Parker
Publisher & C.E.O. - Stuart Levy

Come visit us online at www.TOKYOPOP.com

A **TOKYOPOP** Cine-Manga™
TOKYOPOP Inc.
5900 Wilshire Blvd., Suite 2000, Los Angeles, CA 90036

Spongebob Squarepants: Another Day, Another Sand Dollar

ISBN: 1-59532-209-4
First TOKYOPOP® printing: August 2004

10 9 8 7 6 5 4 3 2 1

Printed in Canada

NICKELODEON

SpongeBob squarepants ™

Created by *Stephen Hillenburg*

ANOTHER DAY, ANOTHER SAND DOLLAR

TOKYOPOP®

HAMBURG · LONDON · LOS ANGELES · TOKYO

SpongeBob™ squarepants

SPONGEBOB SQUAREPANTS: An optimistic and friendly se sponge who lives in a pineapple with his pet snail, Gary, and work as a fry cook a The Krusty Kra He loves his jo and is always looking on the bright side of everything.

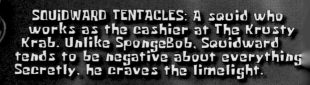

SQUIDWARD TENTACLES: A squid who works as the cashier at The Krusty Krab. Unlike SpongeBob, Squidward tends to be negative about everything Secretly, he craves the limelight.

MR. KRABS: A crab who owns and runs The Krusty Krab. Mr. Krabs loves money and will do anything to avoid losing it. Mr. Krabs also adores his daughter, Pearl.

GARY: SpongeBob's pet snail. Meows like a cat.

PLANKTON: A plankton who constantly sneaks into The Krusty Krab attempting to get his hands on a famous Krusty Krabby Patty. Despite his size, Plankton can be a big threat to Mr. Krabs.

PATRICK STAR: A starfish who is SpongeBob's best friend and neighbor.

SpongeBob™ SquarePants

ANOTHER DAY, ANOTHER SAND DOLLAR

SpongeBob™ SquarePants

Help Wanted

by Stephen Hillenburg, Derek Drymon and Tim Hill

I'M READY!
I'M READY!
I'M READY!

I'M READY!

GO, SPONGEBOB!

I'M READY!
I'M READY!
I'M READY!
I'M READY!

THE FINEST EATING ESTABLISHMENT EVER ESTABLISHED FOR EATING...

THERE IT IS...

THE KRUSTY KRAB. HOME OF THE KRABBY PATTY.

WITH THE "HELP WANTED" SIGN IN THE WINDOW!

HELP WANTED

Bubblestand

by Ennio Torresan, Erik Wiese,
Stephen Hillenburg, Derek Drymon
and Tim Hill

RIGHT...LIKE I WOULD SPEND A MOMENT OF MY TIME... BLOWING BUBBLES.

UH-HUH!

BUBBLES 25¢

I MEAN, WHO IN THE WORLD WOULD PAY TO BLOW BUBBLES?!

GOOD MORNING!

UHHHHH?!

WHOAAA!!!

KRAK!

BAM!

UMMM... OH BOY...

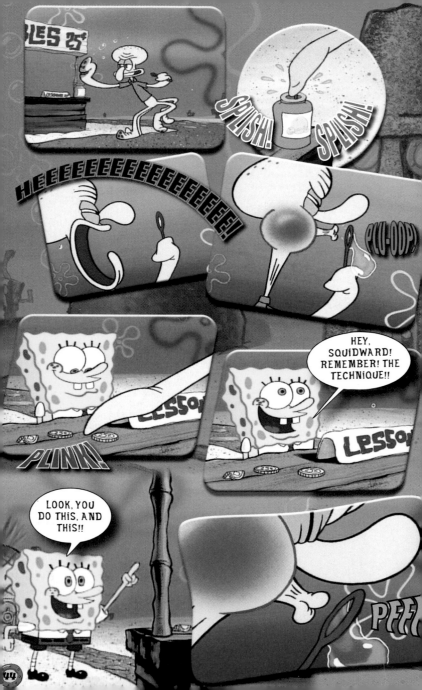

Graveyard Shift

by Mr. Lawrence, Jay Lender and Dan Povenmire

YAAAAAAAAAAAAAAAAAAAAAAAAAA!
AAAAAAAAAAAAAAAAAAAA!
GASP! GASP!
PANT! PANT!
AAAAAAAAAAAAAAAAAAAA!
YOU'RE NOT AFRAID?
PIECE O' CAKE!
SNAP!
WELL, I AM... ESPECIALLY AFTER...WELL... YOU KNOW.
WHAT? WHAT DO I KNOW?
YOU DON'T REMEMBER? IT WAS ALL OVER THE NEWS!

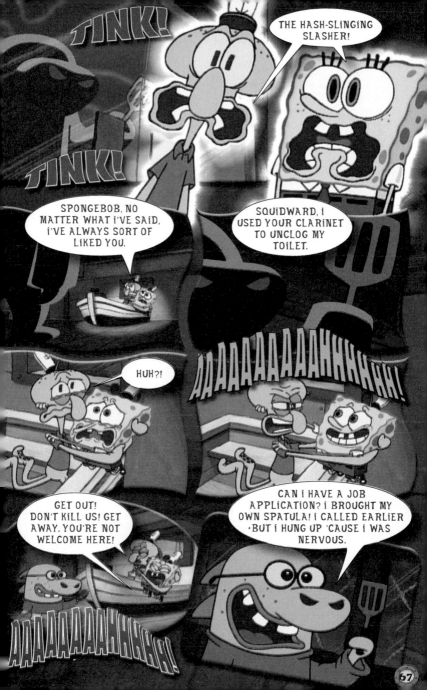

The Fry Cook Games

by Jay Lender, Dan Povenmire
and Merriwether Williams

I'M GONNA GET A JOB AS A FRY COOK AND IT'LL BE EASY!
FINE!
GRRRRR!
KRUSTY...KRAB. KRUSTY...KRAB!! KRUSTY...KRAB!!
KRUSTY...KRAB! KRUSTY...KRAB!
SNIFF!
SNIFF!
I SMELL PLANKTON!
OH YEAH?!

PURE GENIUS!

JIMMY BLASTS OFF
IN HIS OWN CINE-MANGA™

ILABLE NOW!

www.TOKYOPOP.com

93

MANGA

.HACK//LEGEND OF THE TWILIGHT
ANGELIC LAYER
BABY BIRTH
BRAIN POWERED
BRIGADOON
B'TX
CANDIDATE FOR GODDESS, THE
CARDCAPTOR SAKURA
CARDCAPTOR SAKURA - MASTER OF THE CLOW
CHRONICLES OF THE CURSED SWORD
CLAMP SCHOOL DETECTIVES
CLOVER
COMIC PARTY
CORRECTOR YUI
COWBOY BEBOP
COWBOY BEBOP: SHOOTING STAR
CRAZY LOVE STORY
CRESCENT MOON
CROSS
CULDCEPT
CYBORG 009
D•N•ANGEL
DEMON DIARY
DEMON ORORON, THE
DIGIMON
DIGIMON TAMERS
DIGIMON ZERO TWO
DRAGON HUNTER
DRAGON KNIGHTS
DRAGON VOICE
DREAM SAGA
DUKLYON: CLAMP SCHOOL DEFENDERS
ET CETERA
ETERNITY
FAERIES' LANDING
FLCL
FLOWER OF THE DEEP SLEEP
FORBIDDEN DANCE
FRUITS BASKET
G GUNDAM
GATEKEEPERS
GIRL GOT GAME
GIRLS EDUCATIONAL CHARTER
GUNDAM BLUE DESTINY
GUNDAM SEED ASTRAY
GUNDAM WING
GUNDAM WING: BATTLEFIELD OF PACIFISTS
GUNDAM WING: ENDLESS WALTZ
GUNDAM WING: THE LAST OUTPOST (G-UNIT)

HANDS OFF!
HARLEM BEAT
HYPER RUNE
I.N.V.U.
INITIAL D
INSTANT TEEN: JUST ADD NUTS
JING: KING OF BANDITS
JING: KING OF BANDITS - TWILIGHT TALES
JULINE
KARE KANO
KILL ME, KISS ME
KINDAICHI CASE FILES, THE
KING OF HELL
KODOCHA: SANA'S STAGE
LEGEND OF CHUN HYANG, THE
MAGIC KNIGHT RAYEARTH I
MAGIC KNIGHT RAYEARTH II
MAN OF MANY FACES
MARMALADE BOY
MARS
MARS: HORSE WITH NO NAME
MINK
MIRACLE GIRLS
MODEL
MOURYOU KIDEN
MY LOVE
NECK AND NECK
ONE
ONE I LOVE, THE
PEACH GIRL
PEACH GIRL: CHANGE OF HEART
PITA-TEN
PLANET LADDER
PLANETES
PRINCESS AI
PSYCHIC ACADEMY
QUEEN'S KNIGHT, THE
RAGNAROK
RAVE MASTER
REALITY CHECK
REBIRTH
REBOUND
RISING STARS OF MANGA
SAILOR MOON
SAINT TAIL
SAMURAI GIRL REAL BOUT HIGH SCHOOL
SEIKAI TRILOGY, THE
SGT. FROG
SHAOLIN SISTERS
SHIRAHIME-SYO: SNOW GODDESS TALES

NICKELODEON

SpongeBob SquarePants

ALSO AVAILABLE FROM TOKYOPOP®

8675309
BiKiNi BOTTOM
COUNTY JAiL

3
2
1
5
4
3

CRiME AND FUNiSHMENT

8491139

96